**DRIVE TO SURVIVE**

**THINGS YOU SHOULD KNOW BEFORE DRIVING**

Introduction

This book is about driving a vehicle on the highway, city, county or where ever you drive.

It doesn't make any difference what kind of vehicle, what brand of vehicle or what size of vehicle.

It doesn't matter what age you are, what sex you are, or what nation you come from.

This is about driving habits, being considerate on the road, yours and my pet peeves. It is written in a humorous way but the information is very serious.

I hope you enjoy the book, if you see yourself in the book or see others you know who do the things in the book, then I ask you to buy them a copy of the book.

Thank you for taking the time to read it.

If you have a cell phone keep it charged before driving and have it handy, but don't talk/text while driving.

To begin driving in many countries you must first complete some sort of driving course. The course is suppose to train you for driving in all sorts of traffic as well as on many different surfaces. You should receive knowledge of the local traffic laws, what highway symbols mean, what to do in the event of an accident.

You should also learn what are some basic rules of the road; who has the right of way, how far back from a light to stop, what to do at an unmarked railroad crossing, and other matters not covered in manuals.

Unfortunately, not all drivers get the proper information or choose not to obey the rules. Some drivers never got the information because they never took the courses. Some drivers may be to old to remember the rules.

What ever the reason we as drivers must be on constant alert to the other drivers on the road. We must do our part to keep the highways and byways safe for our families and friends.

So lets begin with the basics;

## Chapter One

### Your vehicle

Before you begin driving you should make sure your vehicle is in good running condition. That entails checking the oil level, window washing fluid, and water/anti freeze levels. Next check your belts for worn or frayed spots. Look around the engine area for leaks, loose wires, or broken brackets or clips. Check window wipers, front and back, for wear or tears.

Next we need to check if all are windows and door work properly. On cars with electronic windows, check each button to see if it working. On older cars with wind up windows (I know you younger folks don't know what that is) make sure the crank works. If a door won't open the window is your only other means of escape in the event of an accident. I carry a window breaker in my car just in case the electronics doesn't allow me to get the window down.

Check your tires for proper air pressure. If you don't know the correct pressure check with the dealership or your local tire store. They will often do this for free. You can also look on the tire itself for the proper air pressure. If you have the car manual it will tell you the right pressure for the time of the year. Yes tire pressures vary with the temperature changes. Look at the tread ware to see if the tires need replacement. If you have your oil changed regularly ask them to show you how to measure tire tread ware. Most tires stores will also help you for free.

If you plan to keep your car for awhile try to keep it clean inside and out. Having a dirty vehicle can cause the exterior to become marred or the paint to wear off. The interior carpets and seats will wear out sooner when there is dirt to abrade the fibers.

Okay now that we have covered the pre driving checks lets move on to driving

.

Before starting the car there are a couple of things you should do.

a. Adjust the seat to your comfort level. Check if your legs are close enough to the pedals, is the back in the upright position for the way you sit. Is the seat high enough that you can see over the front of the car.

b. Fasten your seat belt. With most cars today there is an alarm sound to alert you to the fact seat belts are not fastened. Save yourself from a fine an buckle up it's the law.

c. Adjust the rear view mirror as well as the outside mirrors. The outside mirrors should be set so that you can tell if there is a car next to you. In some driving courses they say to be sure to see the grass. It may seem odd at first but it may save your life someday.

d. If you have passengers in your car they need to buckle up as well. Remember it is the law in most states and even in foreign countries.

e. If you have children in the car be sure they are properly buckled in, car seats are turned properly for the age of the child. If you have access to video screens for the back seat check them before and not while driving

f. For the ladies, perform you make up applications before and not while driving.

g. Turn off you phone. Texting or talking while driving could be the last thing you do. If you must leave your phone on pull over to answer an talk. A couple of minutes may save your life and those in the car with you.

## Chapter Two

## On The Road

Now that we are all set to drive let's get on the road.

a. It is just a simple thing but one many people don't do: Look before you begin to pull out. Just because you are on a street with little traffic doesn't mean someone didn't come out of no where while you put the vehicle in drive. (first gear for you with manual transmissions)

b. Signal your intentions. Let other drivers know you plan to pull on to the road. This is not only a being nice but it is the law, who knows it may just save your life.

c. Once you are on the move adjust you speed to the traffic. If you pull out into traffic and don't accelerate the vehicles behind you may not be able to stop before striking you. This does not mean you have to speed just get up to speed quickly. (I'll discuss this more later)

Driving on the highway

1. Driving on the highway has many hazards. Depending on where you drive you will encounter different types of hazards. Be prepared for changes in speed, changes in the weather, night and day driving.

2. Driving on country lanes and dirt roads is far different than on a city street. Those of you who drive on a dirt road know what can happen when the road surface changes form gravel to dirt to mud.

a. Driving on Gravel

The road surface of gravel can be very hazardous. The surface is loose and does not have a good stopping grip. If you go fast on gravel you increase your risk of having an accident. Taking a turn on gravel at high speed will cause your vehicle to slide, more so than on a hard surface. There is a reason that the speed limits are lower on this type surface, it's to help prevent you from having an accident.

Trying to stop at an intersection on a gravel road takes more distance than on a hard surface. The loose impediments do not offer the grip a hard surface would. Slow down when approaching the intersection so that you don't slide through it when you apply the brakes.

Driving on Dirt

Usually a dirt road will have a hard surface, however, the loose dirt on top of the hard surface may cause less grip for your tires.

When taking a turn where there is lots of sand or dirt built up you could slide right through the turn and off the road. The same applies to stopping.

Muddy roads

If the road surface is muddy it may not be passable. If you choose to go through the mud fast you could slide and you could go into the ditch (if there is one).

If you try to go through slow you could become bogged down. (who's going to walk through the mud to get help?

Muddy roads should be avoided if at all possible. Just because someone else drove through the mess doesn't mean you can get through. They may have had four wheel drive or been in a truck with proper tires for the conditions.

Driving on paved roads

Paved surface roads can be a hazard as well. When oil from the road surface builds up it can act like you are on an ice surface and cause your vehicle to slide. If the road surface is broken up with pot holes you could ruin your tire by hitting the holes at high or low speed. Avoiding the holes could also cause you to lose control by turning to fast and over correcting.

Be aware of object on the road that may have fallen from other vehicles. Large trucks often lose a part of their tires. Open trailers have object fly off, and vehicles hauling boats and other recreational items lose thing as well. The best course of action is not to follow too close. Give yourself room to maneuver around the items.

Chapter Three

Winter Driving

Winter driving has its own set of hazards. Most drivers in the northern states know about driving on snow and ice, however, if you live in an area where snow and ice are rare there are thing you need to be aware of.

1. What to do if you start to slide?

a. First thing to do is take your foot off the gas pedal and take your car off cruise.

b. Turn your steering wheel in the direction of the slide/skid. I am often asked why this is done, well, if your tires are turned sideways to the turn you risk catching on an object and flipping over. When your wheels are turned the direction of the slide/skid if you hit and object your chances of flipping are reduced. Also when you hit a dry surface again you want to be going straight.

c. Tap your brake do not slam on your brake. If you have ABS on your car pressing the brake pedal will engage your brakes gradually to slow you down.

d. Try not to panic. Continue to fight for control of your vehicle, having a panic attack will not help.

2. What to do If your vehicle is stuck or disabled.

a. If your vehicle has become stuck or disables by because of an accident, first check for injures to yourself and passengers. If you are the only vehicle involved and have the a method to call for assistance do so.

b. Remain in your car if you are not in danger from the vehicle. If there is a fire hazard exit the vehicle and move away to a safe distance. If the vehicle is in danger of being struck by other vehicles exit the vehicle as soon as possible. Turn on your hazard lights.

c.If you are not able to free your vehicle don't make matters worse by getting it stuck further. Rocking back an forth may work some places but many times it can cause the vehicle to become further mired.

d. If you are not able to reach help immediately get comfortable and hopefully someone will come along. If you are in a remote area and don't think someone will be coming you have a couple of choices. If the weather is bad (snow blowing freezing rain) do not try to walk for help, wait for the weather to improve. More people die from hypothermia while trying to walk for help than if they had remained in the car.

e. If you are involved in a multi vehicle accident there are other concerns you need to be aware of. In an on going crash where vehicles are plowing into one another the safest thing to do, if possible, is exit your vehicle and try to reach a safe place away from the accident.

f. When many vehicles are involved there is always the chance for fire or explosion. Unless you are a trained medical or rescue person do not try to help unless you feel you can do so safely. Many times an untrained individual could cause more damage than good.

g. When winter or cold weather is upon you it is time to consider putting a survival kit in your car. Some items to consider:

First Aid kit Bottled Water

Blanket Flashlight

Gloves Extra Batteries

Warm hat List of Emergency contact numbers

Warm Coat Small shovel

.

3. What to do on winter surfaces?

a. Snow

Driving on snow is better than on an icy surface it will give your tires some grip, however deep snow will bog you down. If the road is plowed it does not mean that it is safe, it is just easier to drive on.

b. Ice

When you encounter ice on the road the first thing you should do is slow down. It is not recommended that you brake suddenly. Let off on the gas and take the vehicle off cruise. (it is never wise to use cruise in bad weather of any kind. When traveling on ice your vehicle will be at the mercy of the conditions. (Winds, vehicles passing, sudden gust) Be aware of other vehicles around you. The other driver may not be as good a driver as you.

c. Black Ice

Black ice is a condition that has caused many accidents. Because it may not be seen until you are already on it you may not become aware of it until it is too late. Moisture on the road freezes in spots and lays in wait for the unsuspecting driver to hit it.

d. Fatigue

Being fatigued when driving anytime should be avoided. Driving fatigue when the road conditions are bad is extremely dangerous. Take frequent breaks to stay alert. Caffeine will help but it has its limits.

## Chapter Four

### Some Things you Need To Know

a. You don't always have the right away.

I have seen many drivers assume they have the right away when entering a major highway from an on ramp. Just because you have your signal light on and you are on the right does not give you the right to pull out into traffic. Those vehicles on the highway have the right away. Sure I know what you're saying "I know that.", but there are still some drivers who don't and you should be aware of them.

b. A stop sign means you are required to stop.

It is for your safety. I see many drivers on the road who brake (or not) but don't stop. They just look and go. Seems harmless if there is no other traffic doesn't it. Until the day when you are looking one way and continuing while a vehicle is coming from the other way at a high rate of speed. Then what? It is a normal practice on country roads because you can see so far and there may be a cloud of dust to alert you of other drivers. Trouble with that is when you get in the city you apply the same habits.

c. When at a four-way stop, three-way stop who has the right of way?

Well the rule of the road says the person to your right has the right of way. Trouble is everybody is to somebody's right. The other rule is the first at the stop has the right of way. Now to set your mind at ease try this; if no one moves begin to move, if someone else moves let them go and then you, the rest will follow.

4. Signal Lights

a. Probably one of the biggest complaints I have about other drivers is their failure to signal their intention. Have you ever been stopped at a signal light waiting for it to turn green and when it does the vehicle across from you decides to turn left. They didn't have a signal light on or they just put it on as they were turning. Don't panic let them go.

Or the guy in front of you wants to turn left but he doesn't indicate it so you wait while the cars from the other side drive by. Then because he didn't move out to make the turn the light changes again and you have to wait some more. Surely that never happens Right?

b. If you are going to change lanes or make a turn from the highway either left or right you are required to signal your intentions. So why is it that so many people ignore the rule.

You are driving on a four lane highway and the vehicle in front of you decides they want to past the vehicle in front of them. Instead of signaling they just pull out causing you to have to brake to avoid them.

Are you angry? Yes.

How about the guy that wants to turn off on the right. Instead of easing up on the gas and falling in behind you they speed up and without signaling they pull in front you and dart down the ramp.

Are You angry? Yes.

I am reminded of the person who chased after a vehicle, that had not signaled, and waved them to stop. When they asked what the problem was he told them their signal light wasn't working. Then got in his vehicle and drove away.

Was he happy? Yes.

Chapter Five

Increased Traffic

Many years ago I noticed the traffic from St Louis eastward was bumper to bumper on most major highways. Now the same is true from Denver eastward.

Why is that important? Semi Tractor and trailers make a large portion of that traffic. Some are pulling two and three trailers at once.

Let's set the scene; There are three semis pulling their load and come to a rise in the road, the one in front is carrying a large load and can't make speed for the rise, The two following are aware of this and must either back off or pass.

Now here comes a little car who is driving the speed limit and decides he wants to pass the slower vehicles. He drives up on the back of the trail vehicle until he has to move out in the passing lane. In the mean time the second truck signals and pulls out to pass. Since the driver of the car is so close to the other truck he doesn't see the driver pull out. Now the driver of the third truck signals his intent to pass. what do you think is going to happen?

Two things the car driver did wrong; they drove to close to the trailing truck, and failed to signal their intent where the truck driver could see him. Secondly not allowing space back from the last truck so that the driver could see them.

Many people are afraid of large trucks on the road. They become frightened when being passed by the large vehicles. It is a fact of the road you will encounter large vehicle on the road so be sure to stay alert around them.

You see not all truck drivers care. In fact many driver have a dislike for small vehicles.

Those large trucks are operating on the principal that time is money. They have a business to run and getting the products to the destination is their only concern.

So here are some hints;

When you are trailing a large truck while you are in the outside lane and he wants to pass, you have two options speed up and pass them or slow down and let them pass.

If your going to pass do so, but don't linger along side the truck, speed up and pass.

I prefer to let them pullout and pass, they have a schedule I don't. I will often flash my lights to let them know it is safe to pull out then I wait until they complete their pass then flash my lights again to let them know it is safe to pull back in.

Remember, large vehicles need space to make turns, don't pass on the right if they pull out to make a right hand turn.

It is not only trucks that are a hazard on the road cars, buses and large recreational vehicles as well as vehicles pulling trailers or boats are also.

One of the things that irritates me is when a car decides to pass me but lingers in my blind spot. Has that ever happened to you? The passing vehicle is fencing you in so you have to adjust your speed so as not to tail gate the vehicle in front of you.

## Chapter Six

## Driving With Occupants

Driving with people in the vehicle.

One of the big no no's of driving with someone else in the vehicle is having an argument while driving. I don't know anyone who can have an argument with someone without looking at them. If you use your hands to talk it is even worse. Just don't do it. Taking your eyes off the road can result in an accident in seconds.

Children in the back seat.

Unless you have trained your children extremely well there will be distractions from children. I think one of the best thing they did was put video players in the back so kids will sit quietly and watch. That's not to say they still won't cause a disturbance.

Dads can usually stem the activity easier than moms but not always. There is no quick cure for this problem if there were the inventor would make millions. Should the distraction become to much, my solution is to stop and wait till they settle down enough to allow you to drive with your mind on the road.

We all know what a backseat driver is.

It is not just your mother in law. Anyone who has to deal with a backseat driver can become distracted from driving by the continued harangue from a backseat driver. The backseat driver is not always in the back seat.

Is there a solution, I doubt it. If it won't get your fired, divorced or arrested Tell them to please be quiet so you can drive without distraction, good luck.

## Chapter Seven

## The Old And The New

How many of you remember the button on the floor that dimmed your lights? Having a push button start? Using a crank? Using your arm to signal a turn? Having a clutch pedal?

Over the 100 plus years cars and truck have been around they have changed drastically wouldn't you agree?

Today's vehicle drive systems and engines are so confusing that even trained mechanics have difficulty working on them.

You may still be able to change your own oil and filter, but with the cost of the oil and the filter and disposing of the old oil correctly, it is just as cheap to have it done If there is a sale on even better.

Car makers have used a color code to point out the different fluid check and fill points. The color yellow usually indicates something you can do yourself. The four things that come to mind are:

Check or fill the engine oil.

Check and fill the brake fluid.

Check and fill the coolant.

Check and fill The washer fluids

Fortunately all these thing and more can be done at no charge. Most of the major auto supply stores offer their customers free checks. They will also replace your windshield wiper blades, loan you a tool while at the store, check your tire pressure and give you instruction on what you can do yourself.

Tire stores will also check you air pressure and even measure your thread life and make a recommendation on replacement. There may still be unscrupulousness dealers, however if they want your repeat business they will treat you right. Even if you are a female.

Getting your vehicle serviced is not the same as having work done on your car. Every time I take my vehicles in for service they do a safety check. If your service person doesn't do one change your service provider.

I don't always make the changes that are recommended. They dealership, if that is where you go, is simply pointing out area's of concern. What you do about them is your decision.

A safety check is not the same as a diagnostic check. Years ago a good mechanic could listen to the motor and tell you what was wrong. Today it requires a computer to diagnose your problems. That's not to say someone familiar with motors can't change your spark plus, if you have any, or replace a belt. If major work needs to be done leave it to the trained mechanic.

Chapter Eight

Maintaining Your Vehicle

A Clean car last longer.

It may not seem that a little dust on the car is going to hurt so we leave it on. Over time the dust and dirt will wear on the paint. When the paint has lost it's protective coat it will begin to fade.

The coastal states and cold weather states face another problem, salt. The seas have salt in them and when the vehicles are sprayed with the sea air the salt covers the car and will begin to corrode the paint and the metal. The same is true with vehicles driving in areas where they use salt to keep ice off the road.

It is a wise driver that takes the time to at least wash off the dirt and salt as soon as they have a chance. Using the numerous car washes, automatic wash or do it yourself may seem a waste of time but you will be glad you did in the long run.

Another item to take note of is the small chips to the paint you vehicle gets from rocks and other items hitting you. If your destination takes you on an unpaved road you will encounter loose rock and debris.

If you live in the rural area your chances are higher that you will encounter many forms of debris.

Two things that I had done to my truck when I bought it were to seal the under side of the truck and to spray the truck bed with a protective coating. Not everyone can afford to do this I know. An alternative is to cover the bed or install a bed liner. Having a bed lined with something will help prevent dents and scrapes that could lead to rusting.

Chapter Nine

Safety

Lets talk a little about safety.

I know I mention this earlier when talking about road conditions. Now I want to talk about other safety tips.

If your travel time includes the hours just before dusk or dawn your chances of encountering wild life are greater. Should the area you are passing through be wooded or near open fields you should remain very aware of wild life crossing the road. That's not to say you won't encounter animals in other areas, they may just be smaller.

During the rutting season for deer the odds are greater that you will see them crossing the highway. There is a saying that if you see one deer there are others near by.

When the deer come out to feed at night they are very nervous and the slightest movement will send them running. The fences along the highway are not for the deer, as they can jump over fences twenty feet high. Those fences are to keep farm animals in and even they will get out.

Deer are often chased by coyotes and other predatory animals so if a deer is running you should be alert to a trailing animal.

Deer are not the only animal that cause accidents. If you were to see a skunk on the road would you run over it? How about an armadillo any other small creature?

Avoiding animals in the road is a common driving hazard. While you swerve to miss the animal your chances of loosing control increase. If you can slow down an avoid the animal safely well and good. If you are traveling to fast to stop it may be better to strike the animal rather than risk having an accident. Sounds cruel but it could mean their life or yours or your loved ones.

So We have covered the deer and the small animals what's next. How about flying objects and non flying fowl?

I once crested a hill and found a flock of ten turkeys in the middle of the road. I sounded my horn to attempt to scare them but they ignored me. I slowed down and when I reached them they moved off to the side.

Chickens and all farm animals that are not in a cage can be found roaming on the roads in the rural areas. You may have heard the question; Why did the chicken cross the road? Because it was there.

Most people who live in the farming communities are aware of the hazards of farm animals running loose. You city folk may not even know what the animal is.

Have you ever had a bird fly into your windshield? Scary isn't it. Even large bugs give me a fright. The large birds that are to slow to avoid a speeding car can turn a windscreen into a mess of cracks causing you to lose sight of the road. I know you city folk don't face this problem in the urban areas but you might drive in the country someday so be aware.

No matter where you drive there will be the danger of striking an object. If the hazard is there slow down until you pass it.

Chapter Ten

Rules And Signs

Rules and signs that may save a life.

Knowing the meaning of road signs is required for passing your driving test. Not all signs are in the driving test book so learn them on the road and obey them.

School Crossing:

This is a reminder that small children are using this path to cross the street. It may not have a traffic light or a crossing guard. It is your responsibility to slow down and be aware of children crossing the road.

School Bus Stop Sign:

On the side of all school buses they have a stop sign which is deployed whenever the bus is picking up or dropping off students. By Law you may not pass this vehicle on either side until the sign has been retracted. Even then be wary that a child might still try to cross after the bus has gone. Remember as well that school buses stop at railroad crossings.

Curve and ramp speeds.

When you see a speed sign as you approach a curve or a ramp it is there to recommend the speed that you should use while negotiating the turn or ramp. If the weather conditions are bad then slowing down to the recommended speed could save your life.

Construction Zones

Every effort should be made to avoid striking road workers. Flag persons are there for a reason. Not only do you risk a fine that will be doubled you risk taking a

Traveling in a construction zone, even when there are no workers, you are required to obey the posted speed limit. You could encounter objects in the road or different road levels. There are often loose impediments that could fly up from the vehicle in front of you. So slow down and live and save the life of another.

Railroad Crossings

This week in the news I saw three separate accidents involving trains. One took the life of 6 teenagers. The crossing guards and the lights are there for a reason. Not only is it a law to obey them it could save your life.

If you approach a railroad crossing that has no lights or crossing guards it doesn't mean it is safe to cross. Stop and look BOTH ways before crossing. The sound a train makes is not always heard from a distance. If you have noise in your vehicle you may not hear a train until it is right on you. Be safe and don't tempt fate.

Cars Entering from the side

I believe that many people that drive have lost the ability to use common sense. Or don't have any to begin with.

When I drive on a major road I know I am suppose to move over to the other lane to allow the drivers entering the roadway to move on the road. It's the law.

But what if I have a car or truck next to me and can't move over. What if there is a car passing me or tail gating me and I can't slow down. That driver entering the road does not have the right of way!

When entering on to the highway from an on ramp you must allow for those vehicles already on the highway. You are the one who must wait until you can safely enter on the road. You are the one responsible to maintain a safe speed after you are on the road. You are the one responsible for signaling your intention to enter the highway. If the traffic does not allow you to enter you must wait until you can safely get on the highway and not force your vehicle into traffic.

Traffic Speeds

In Germany and Italy I drove on the autobahn and the auto-strata, major roads in those countries. It was not a law that I knew of but it was a rule of the road that if a car was coming up fast in your lane and flashed its lights you moved out of the way. Speed limits in many places were not used or didn't exist.

I drove a Fiat, no match for the BMW's and the Mercedes and the Ferrari. Today they have put some restrictions on speed, but the flashing lights still mean the same.

On the highways in most states the maximum speed ranges from 55 to 80. The speeds on the rural roads range from 40 to 65. Depending on the state and the cities. Usually in town speeds go no higher that 30 to 40

So what happens is people take the maximum speed and add 5 and that is the speed they feel they can get away with so they don't get a ticket. You know what; they are usually right.

I drive many hours on the highways with my speed kept to the limit or just over it by a mile or two and I set my cruise. At this speed I have become an impediment to other drivers. I often wonder why the other vehicles that pass me and then pass by a police vehicle running radar that they are not stopped.

With today's cars and trucks running at high speed is still a danger. Think about it; driving at 75 instead of 85 is only ten miles faster but it takes ten car links more to stop. If a truck is running at top speed and you pull in front of them and reduce your speed the vehicle may not be able to slow to your lower speed and could run over you. Can you control a spin on ice better at 80 than at 75?

Folks speed kills it's a fact. Do you know that if I drive at 60 miles an hour and you drive at 65 you only gain 5 minute an hour to our destination. Is your life and that of others worth that five minutes?

Passing

How far back is a safe distance to the vehicle in front of you. If you are traveling at 75 how quickly will you stop before striking the vehicle in front of you?

The rule I use is for every ten mile I am driving I need that many car lengths from the leading car.

If I wish to pass the vehicle in front of me I don't wait until I am a car length behind to pull out and pass. Signal and pull out so the other driver is aware of your passing and doesn't suddenly pull out in front of you.There are exceptions. When you are boxed in and have to slow until you are able to pass, or the vehicle is slowing to make a turn

When you decide to make a pass there are thing you need to consider; Is there room for me to pass safely, can I go fast enough to make the pass safely, Are there changes in the road ahead that could effect my passing. Are there other cars they may pull out to pass as well.

When you pass be sure that you signal your intentions before you pull to the passing lane. When you complete your pass signal you intent to pull back in. After you have made the pass turn off your signal light.

Making Turns

No matter what turn you plan to make be sure to signal your intent well enough in advance to notify the vehicles behind you.

I can't count the times I have seen a vehicle make a turn and wait till the last second to signal.

How about the vehicle that is waiting for the light to change and doesn't signal their intent to turn. I suppose you are supposed to guess their intent.

Then there is the guy who made a turn two blocks back but forgot his signal light was on so you slow up waiting for him to turn at every cross road.

If you are the one who forgets then think how the other person feels about you.

Emergency vehicle

When an emergency vehicle is flashing it's light or has the siren going you are required to pull to the side of the road no matter which direction it is coming from, until it passes and no other emergency vehicles are coming.

What if there is no room to pull over? Then move over as far as safely possible an stop until they pass. You will probably make the drivers behind you upset if they don't want to follow the law, so what.

Out of respect for the dead, when a funeral possession passes it is customary to pull over until they pass.

## Chapter 11

## Avoidance

Things to avoid while driving

Don't drink and drive, use a designated driver. A buzz feeling is just as bad as being wasted.

Don't drive while under the influence of drugs. All drugs alter the body in some way. The medication you get from a doctor may say do not drive while taking this medication. There is a reason for that.

Avoid driving while sleepy or tired. Your eyes may droop or close involuntarily. Take frequent breaks to get fresh air and stretch.

Don't drive angry.

When you are angry you will have a tendency to go faster and your reaction time is slower. Calm down and live.

Don't drive if your vehicle is unsafe.

If you have a light that is not working, or a horn not working or signal lights not working or anything else that could be hazardous to driving.

I'm reminded of the friend that was stopped for driving under the influence. He complained to the officer that he wasn't speeding or doing anything bad. The officer said," You have a head light out." Had he fixed it before hand he might have avoided the expense of the ticket.

Don't drive when your vision is impaired.

If you are required to wear glasses do so. If your rear view is blocked in the vehicle be sure you have a way to see behind you with side mirrors.

If you drive a large vehicle such as a truck or recreational vehicle be aware of the height of the vehicle. Not all overpasses are the same. Fast food drive thru and gas stations may not accommodate your vehicle.

I am reminded of the driver of a recreational vehicle that sued the manufacturer of the vehicle and won. She had put her vehicle on cruise control and went in to fix herself a sandwich. There was no warning that the vehicle didn't drive itself.

Chapter 12

Other Hazards

There are not just cars and trucks on the road. In some areas of some states there could be a horse and buggy. Some places allow golf carts on the road. Bicycles are becoming more plentiful on rural and mountain roads. Horse back riders sometimes use the highways.

Any time you come across something other than a car or truck they have the right of way. often you will see signs indicating that you should be aware there are one of these types of transportation in the area.

When you are dealing with live animals on the roadway consider this: they can't talk, they are big, they will damage your vehicle, You could be made to pay for their loss.

Other motorized vehicles are governed by the same rules of the road that you are. However use some common sense, give them room.

When you encounter bicycles or motorbikes, or motorcycles give them room to maneuver. They may attempt to pass in between you and another vehicle. Blowing your horn will only startle them and could cause an accident.

Pedestrians in crosswalks always have the right of way,

Children are small and have no sense of where they are

To the other driver, it is you who is the idiot

Don't be the cause of an accident stay alert

I hope you have enjoyed reading this book. I have enjoyed writing it. If you liked this you may enjoy my other books:


Everything you wanted to know about golf but didn't know who to ask.


Did you get my email?


The Drug Fighting Group

www.ingramcontent.com/pod-product-compliance
Lightning Source LLC
Chambersburg PA
CBHW081546280526
45788CB00010B/3364